Termites

by Mari C. Schuh

Consulting Editor: Gail Saunders-Smith, Ph.D.

Consultant: Gary A. Dunn, Director of Education,
Young Entomologists' Society

Pebble Boo

an imprint of Capstone
Mankato, Minnesot

Pebble Books are published by Capstone Press
151 Good Counsel Drive, P.O. Box 669, Mankato, Minnesota 56002
http://www.capstone-press.com

1 2 3 4 5 6 08 07 06 05 04 03

Library of Congress Cataloging-in-Publication Data
Schuh, Mari C., 1975–
    Termites / by Mari C. Schuh.
    p. cm.—(Insects)
    Summary: Simple text and photographs present the physical characteristics,
behavior, and habitat of termites.
    Includes bibliographical references (p. 23) and index.
    ISBN 0-7368-1667-4 (hardcover)
    1. Termites—Juvenile literature. [1. Termites.] I. Title. II. Insects
(Mankato, Minn.)
QL529 .S37 2003
595.7′36—dc21
                                                                    2002007613

Note to Parents and Teachers

The Insects series supports national science standards for units on
the diversity and unity of life. The series shows that animals have
features that help them live in different environments. This book
describes and illustrates termites and their parts and habits. The
photographs support early readers in understanding the text. The
repetition of words and phrases helps early readers learn new
words. This book also introduces early readers to subject-specific
vocabulary words, which are defined in the Words to Know section.
Early readers may need assistance to read some words and to use
the Table of Contents, Words to Know, Read More, Internet Sites,
and Index/Word List sections of the book.

Termites have a soft body and a thick waist.

Table of Contents

Termites 5

What Termites Do. 11

What Termites Eat. 21

Words to Know 22

Read More 23

Internet Sites. 23

Index/Word List. 24

*This book was a gift
to our library
from Capstone Press.*

Termites have
two straight antennas.

wings

Adult termites have
two pairs of wings.

10

Termites live in colonies.

Adult termites fly away from their colony.

The queen termite
lays many eggs. A
new colony begins.

Some termites build nests
and mounds in the soil.

18

Some termites build nests in wood.

20

Most termites eat wood.
They break down dead
wood. They can destroy
houses and trees.

Words to Know

antenna—a feeler on an insect's head

colony—a group of insects that live and work together; as many as two million termites can live in a colony.

destroy—to ruin something so that it cannot be used; termites can destroy houses by eating the wood.

nest—a place that termites or other animals make to live in; termites live, work, and raise young termites in nests.

queen—a female termite whose job is to lay eggs

waist—the middle part of an insect's body

wing—a body part that helps an insect fly; adult termites have four wings that are the same size and length; termites make only one flight in their lifetime; they break off their wings after they fly so that they can crawl more easily.

Read More

Hartley, Karen, Chris Macro, and Philip Taylor. *Termite.* Bug Books. Des Plaines, Ill.: Heinemann Library, 1999.

Squire, Ann. *Termites.* True Books. New York: Children's Press, 2003.

Telford, Carole, and Rod Theodorou. *Through a Termite City.* Amazing Journeys. Des Plaines, Ill.: Heinemann Interactive Library, 1998.

Internet Sites

Track down many sites about termites.
Visit the FACT HOUND at *http://www.facthound.com*

IT IS EASY! IT IS FUN!

1) Go to *http://www.facthound.com*

2) Type in: 0736816674

3) Click on "FETCH IT" and FACT HOUND will find several links hand-picked by our editors.

Relax and let our pal FACT HOUND do the research for you!

23

Index/Word List

adult, 9, 13
antennas, 7
body, 5
break, 21
build, 17, 19
colony, 11,
  13, 15
destroy, 21
eat, 21

eggs, 15
fly, 13
houses, 21
lays, 15
live, 11
mounds, 17
nests, 17, 19
pairs, 9
queen, 15

soft, 5
soil, 17
straight, 7
thick, 5
trees, 21
two, 7, 9
waist, 5
wings, 9
wood, 19, 21

Word Count: 72
Early-Intervention Level: 10

Editorial Credits

Jennifer VanVoorst, editor; Timothy Halldin, series designer; Gene Bentdahl and
  Molly Nei, book designers; Karrey Tweten, photo researcher

Photo Credits

Corbis/George D. Lepp, 1, 4; Gallo Images/Anthony Bannister, 14
James P. Rowan, 8, 10, 18
Jim Kalisch, cover, 6
Photovault.com/Nikko de Rohan, 16
Unicorn Stock Photos/Arthur Gurmankin/Mary Morina, 12; Tommy Dodson, 20